Tools Tell the Weather

Callie Frampton

ROSEN
COMMON CORE
READERS

Rosen Classroom™

New York

Published in 2013 by The Rosen Publishing Group, Inc.
29 East 21st Street, New York, NY 10010

Book Design: Michael Harmon

Photo Credits: Cover Ron Hilton/Shutterstock.com; p. 4 (field) Elnamiv/Shutterstock.com; p. 4 (umbrella) knin/Shutterstock.
com; p. 5 © iStockphoto.com/mikespics; p. 6 (wind sock) Daniela Sachsenheimer/Shutterstock.com;
p. 6 (thermometer) Vasiliy Koval/Shutterstock.com; pp. 6, 18 (rain gauge) Kevin Carden/Shutterstock.com; p. 7 Boston
Globe/Contributor/Boston Globe/Getty Images; pp. 8, 10 Barry Blackburn/Shutterstock.com; p. 9 ChameleonsEye/
Shutterstock.com; p. 11 Nick Caloyianis/National Geographic/Getty Images; p. 12 Doug Allan/Science Photo Library/Getty
Images; p. 13 Medioimages/Photodisc/Thinkstock.com; p. 14 Stephen Aaron Rees/
Shutterstock.com; p. 15 Bruce Works/Shutterstock.com; p. 16 manfredxy/Shutterstock.com; p. 17 Ak W./
Shutterstock.com; p. 19 ZenShui/Sigrid Olsson/PhotoAlto Agency RF Collections/Getty Images; p. 20 Carolina K. Smith,
M.D./Shutterstock.com; p. 21 nito/Shutterstock.com.

ISBN: 978-1-4488-8800-9
6-pack ISBN: 978-1-4488-8801-6

Manufactured in the United States of America

CPSIA Compliance Information: Batch #WS12RC: For further information contact Rosen Publishing, New York, New York at 1-800-237-9932.

Word Count: 361

Contents

Measuring the Weather

Some days, you wake up and it's sunny. Other days, it's rainy. It's easy to see the weather with your eyes.

Sometimes we use tools to tell us about the weather.

The tools tell us things we can't see.

Tools help us know what the weather will be like tomorrow. Some tools are really big. Others can fit in your hand!

Some people study the weather for their job. They use tools to learn about the weather.

Thermometers

A **thermometer** is a weather tool. A thermometer tells us the **temperature**. You can use a thermometer inside or outside.

Some thermometers are long. They're filled with red **liquid**. The higher the red is, the hotter it is.

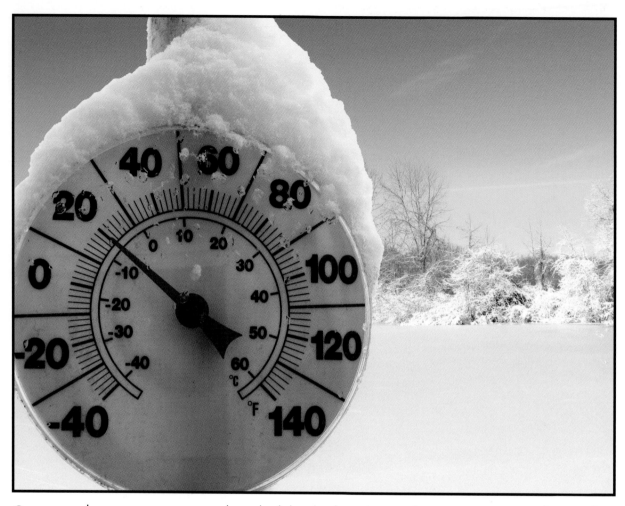

Some thermometers look like clocks. They're round and have a hand. The hand points to the temperature.

Weather Balloons

Sometimes, we study the temperature up in the sky.

We use weather balloons to help us.

Weather balloons carry thermometers high into the air. We read the temperature when the balloon comes back down.

Measuring the Wind

Sometimes we want to study the wind. We want to know which way it blows.

A wind vane tells us the wind's direction. The wind makes the wind vane turn. It points north, south, east, or west.

A wind vane sits on top of a tall building. Sometimes, people put them on their house. You might see one on top of a barn.

Sometimes, the wind blows very hard. We use a tool to **measure** how fast it blows. We put the tool on top of a tall building. The tool has little cups on it.

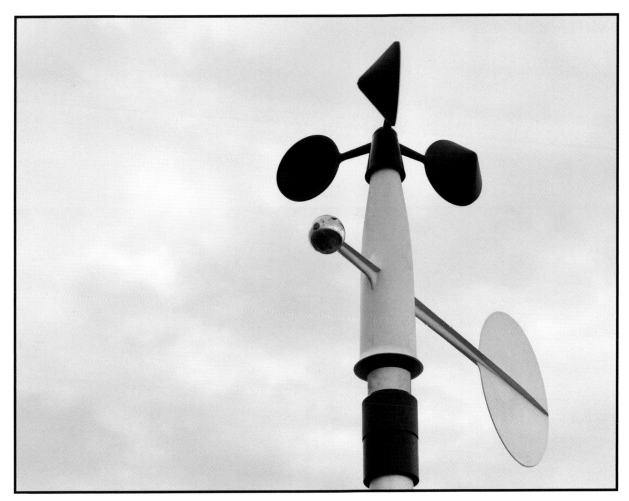

The wind makes the cups spin. The cups spin fast when it's windy. They spin slowly if the wind is light.

Rain Gauges

Another tool we use is called a rain **gauge**. It measures how much rain has fallen. This helps us study Earth.

A rain gauge goes outside. It fills with water when it rains. We measure how high the water is when it stops raining.

Learning About Weather

People like to learn about the weather. Sometimes, we see it on TV. We also read about it in the newspaper.

The weather changes a lot. Tools make it easy
to measure the weather!

Weather Tools

thermometer

Tells us how hot or cold it is.

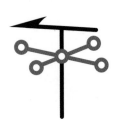

wind vane

Tells us the direction of the wind.

rain gauge

Tells us how much rain has fallen.

Glossary

gauge (GAYJ) A tool used to measure something.

liquid (LIH-kwuhd) Something that flows like water.

measure (MEH-zhuhr) To find the size or number of something.

temperature (TEHM-puhr-chuhr) How hot or cold something is.

thermometer (thuhr-MAH-muh-tuhr) A tool used to measure how hot or cold something is.

Index